CLEVELAND BROWNS

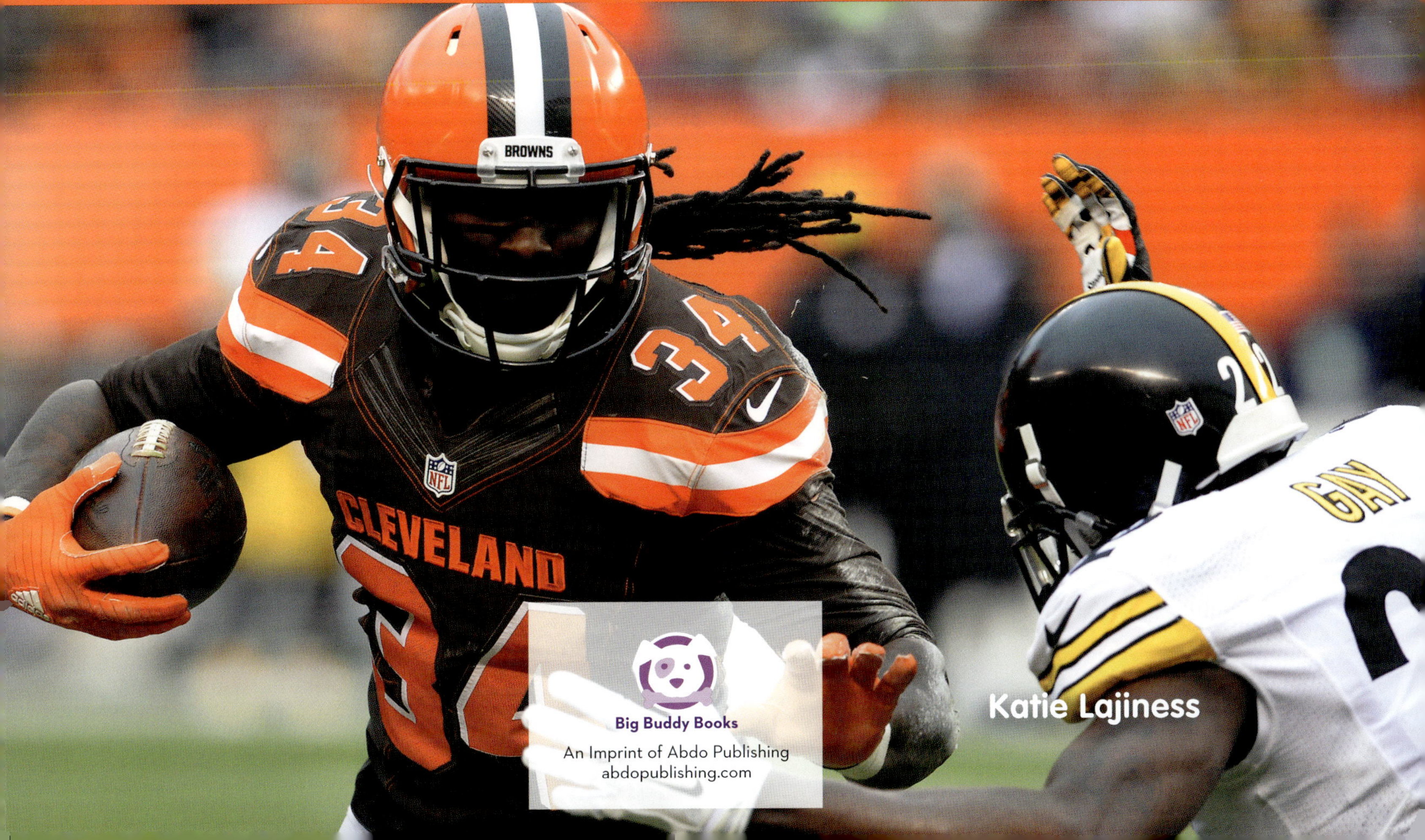

Katie Lajiness

Big Buddy Books
An Imprint of Abdo Publishing
abdopublishing.com

abdopublishing.com

Published by Abdo Publishing, a division of ABDO, PO Box 398166, Minneapolis, Minnesota 55439.

Printed in the United States of America, North Mankato, Minnesota.
092016
012017

Cover Photo: ASSOCIATED PRESS.
Interior Photos: ASSOCIATED PRESS (pp. 5, 7, 9, 13, 14, 17, 18, 19, 20, 21, 22, 23, 24, 25, 27 28, 29); Tony Tomsic (p. 11).

Coordinating Series Editor: Tamara L. Britton
Graphic Design: Michelle Labatt, Taylor Higgins, Jenny Christensen

Publisher's Cataloging-in-Publication Data

Names: Lajiness, Katie, author.
Title: Cleveland Browns / by Katie Lajiness.
Description: Minneapolis, MN : Abdo Publishing, 2017. | Series: NFL's greatest teams | Includes bibliographical references and index.
Identifiers: LCCN 2016944878 | ISBN 9781680785326 (lib. bdg.) | ISBN 9781680798920 (ebook)
Subjects: LCSH: Cleveland Browns (Football team)--History--Juvenile literature.
Classification: DDC 796.332--dc23
LC record available at http://lccn.loc.gov/2016944878

Contents

A Winning Team

The Cleveland Browns are a football team from Cleveland, Ohio. They have played in the National Football League (NFL) for almost 70 years.

The Browns have had good seasons and bad. But time and again, they've proven themselves. Let's see what makes the Browns one of the NFL's greatest teams.

Brown, orange, and white are the team's colors.

THOMAS
73
BROWNS

League Play

The NFL got its start in 1920. Its teams have changed over the years. Today, there are 32 teams. They make up two conferences and eight divisions.

The Browns play in the North Division of the American Football Conference (AFC). This division also includes the Baltimore Ravens, the Cincinnati Bengals, and the Pittsburgh Steelers.

The Cincinnati Bengals have long been a rival of the Browns. Both teams are from Ohio.

Team Standings

The AFC and the National Football Conference (NFC) make up the NFL. Each conference has a north, south, east, and west division.

Kicking Off

The Browns were founded in 1944 by Arthur B. McBride. The team was one of the first in the All-American Football Conference (AAFC).

The Browns were very successful. They won the AAFC **championship** four years in a row! However, the conference ended after the 1949 season. Then the Browns joined the NFL.

The 1948 team went 15–0 that season. The Browns beat the Buffalo Bills to win the championship.

The Name Game

The team's name honors its first coach, Paul Brown.

Highlight Reel

The Browns played their first NFL game on September 16, 1950. They played the NFL **champion** Philadelphia Eagles. The Browns easily beat the Eagles 35–10. They went on to win the championship that season.

From there, the Browns continued their commanding play. From 1951 to 1964, the team played in the NFL championship game seven times. They won it in 1954, 1955, and 1964.

Win or Go Home

NFL teams play 16 regular season games each year. The teams with the best records are part of the play-off games. Play-off winners move on to the conference championships. Then, conference winners face off in the Super Bowl!

The Browns beat the Baltimore Colts 27–0 in the 1964 NFL championship game!

In 1980, many of the team's wins were decided by one touchdown or less. Fans were excited and nervous to see if the Browns would win.

In 1995, owner Art Modell wanted to move his team. Browns fans were very angry! But, the Cleveland Browns moved to Maryland and became the Baltimore Ravens.

Cleveland did not have a football team for three years. During that time the city built a new stadium. Then in 1999, a new NFL team began to play as the Browns.

A bridge connects the stadium to downtown Cleveland. It is decorated to look like a football field.

Still Waiting

As of 2016, the Browns are one of four NFL teams to never have played in a Super Bowl.

Halftime! Stat Break

Team Records

RUSHING YARDS

Career: Jim Brown, 12,312 yards (1957–1965)

Single Season: Jim Brown, 1,863 yards (1963)

PASSING YARDS

Career: Brian Sipe, 23,713 yards (1974–1983)

Single Season: Brian Sipe, 4,132 yards (1980)

RECEPTIONS

Career: Ozzie Newsome, 662 receptions (1978–1990)

Single Season: Ozzie Newsome, 89 receptions (1983, 1984); Kellen Winslow, 89 receptions (2006)

ALL-TIME LEADING SCORER

Lou Groza, 1,608 points (1946–1967)

Fan Fun

STADIUM: FirstEnergy Stadium

LOCATION: Cleveland, Ohio

MASCOTS: Chomps and Swagger

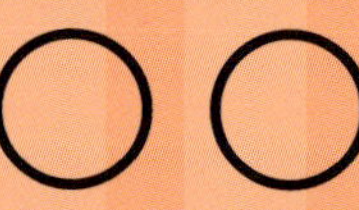

Famous Coaches

Paul Brown (1946–1962)
Blanton Collier (1963–1970)

Championships

EARLY CHAMPIONSHIP WINS:
1946, 1947, 1948, 1949, 1950, 1954, 1955, 1964
SUPER BOWL APPEARANCES:
None
SUPER BOWL WINS:
None

Pro Football Hall of Famers & Their Years with the Browns

Jim Brown, Fullback (1957–1965)
Paul Brown, Coach (1946–1962)
Joe DeLamielleure, Guard (1980–1984)
Len Ford, Defensive End (1950–1957)
Frank Gatski, Center (1946–1956)
Otto Graham, Quarterback (1946–1955)
Lou Groza, Offensive Tackle/Placekicker (1946–1959, 1961–1967)
Gene Hickerson, Guard (1958–1973)
Leroy Kelly, Running Back (1964–1973)
Dante Lavelli, End (1946–1956)
Mike McCormack, Tackle (1954–1962)
Bobby Mitchell, Wide Receiver/Halfback (1958–1961)
Marion Motley, Fullback (1946–1953)
Ozzie Newsome, Tight End (1978–1990)
Paul Warfield, Wide Receiver (1964–1969, 1976–1977)
Bill Willis, Middle Guard (1946–1953)

Coaches' Corner

Paul Brown was the team's first coach. Many people believe he is one of the best NFL coaches in history.

Brown created a coaching style that is still used today. He hired full-time staff to help coach and look for new players.

Brown made his players study film clips. Then, he would test them on what they had seen! During his 17 years with the Browns, they won seven **championships**.

Brown joined the Pro Football Hall of Fame in 1967.

Star Players

Otto Graham QUARTERBACK (1946–1955)

Otto Graham was the first player to sign with the Browns. As quarterback, he led the team to four AAFC and three NFL **championships**. Graham was named Most Valuable Player (MVP) three times. In 1965, he became the first Browns player in the Pro Football Hall of Fame.

Lou Groza OFFENSIVE TACKLE/PLACEKICKER (1946–1959, 1961–1967)

Lou Groza joined the Browns in 1946. During his 21 years with the team he scored 1,608 points. That is a team record! Groza was chosen to play in the Pro Bowl, which is the NFL's all-star game, nine times. And, he won NFL Player of the Year in 1954.

Jim Brown FULLBACK (1957–1965)

Jim Brown was a star player from the start! He was named NFL **Rookie** of the Year in 1957. Brown was also named the NFL's MVP four times. He set many NFL and team records during his **career**. A player once said Brown was "Superman on a football field."

Leroy Kelly RUNNING BACK (1964–1973)

When Leroy Kelly joined the team in 1964, Jim Brown became his **mentor**. When Brown **retired** two years later, Kelly became the team's star ball carrier. Kelly won NFL rushing titles in 1967 and 1968. He joined the Pro Football Hall of Fame in 1994.

Ozzie Newsome TIGHT END (1978–1990)

Ozzie Newsome was nicknamed Wizard of Oz because he rarely dropped a pass. He was a key player who helped the Browns reach the AFC **championship** three times. When Newsome retired in 1990, he had 7,980 **career** receiving yards. That is a team record!

Bernie Kosar QUARTERBACK (1985–1993)

Bernie Kosar was the team's first choice in the 1985 **draft**. In 1986, Kosar set an NFL play-off record. He passed for 489 yards to beat the New York Jets 23–20. It was the team's first play-off win since 1969. From 1990 to 1991, he set another NFL record by throwing 308 passes without an **interception**.

Joe Thomas OFFENSIVE TACKLE (2007–)

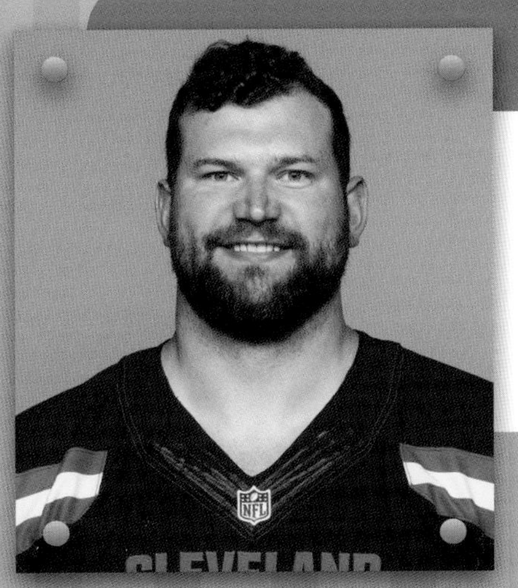

The Browns picked Joe Thomas in the first round of the 2007 draft. In 2014, Thomas made NFL history. He became the first offensive lineman to be named to the Pro Bowl in each of his first eight years.

FirstEnergy Stadium

The Browns play home games at FirstEnergy Stadium. It is in Cleveland. The stadium opened in 1999. It was redone in 2014. FirstEnergy Stadium holds about 67,000 people.

Cleveland's Municipal Stadium opened in 1931. The Browns played there from 1946 to 1995.

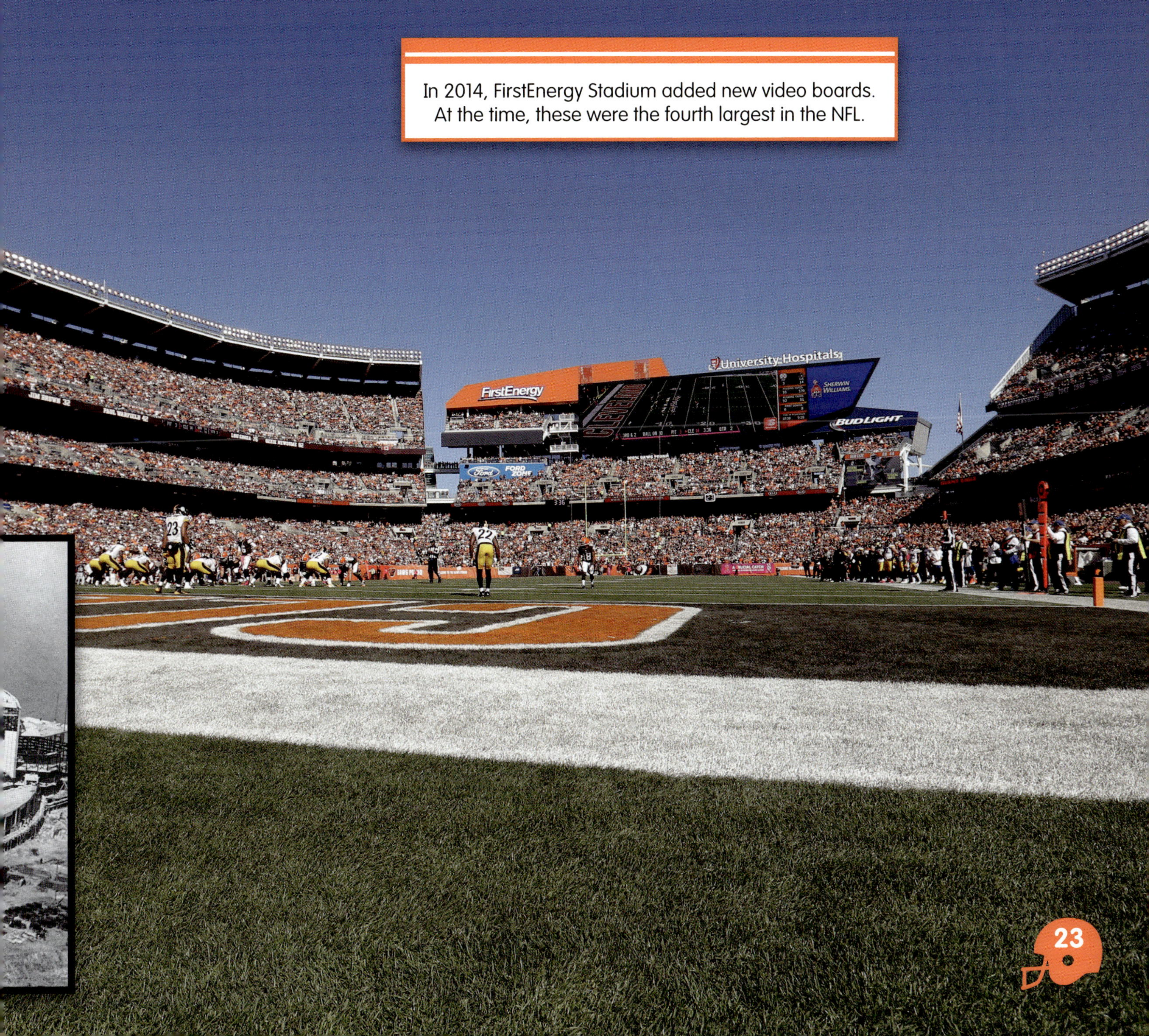

In 2014, FirstEnergy Stadium added new video boards. At the time, these were the fourth largest in the NFL.

Dawg Pound!

Thousands of fans flock to FirstEnergy Stadium to see the Browns play home games. The team's wild fans are part of the Dawg Pound.

Chomps and Swagger are the team's **mascots**. Chomps is a costumed Labrador retriever. Swagger is a live bullmastiff. They help fans cheer on the Browns.

Swagger sits outside his dog house during home games. Off the field, he visits radio stations and team events.

Chomps wears a jersey with the number 00. His favorite song is "Bad to the Bone!"

Some Browns fans wear wacky outfits to the games!

Final Call

The Browns have a long, rich history. They have won eight **championships**.

Even during losing seasons, true fans have stuck by them. Many believe the Cleveland Browns will remain one of the greatest teams in the NFL.

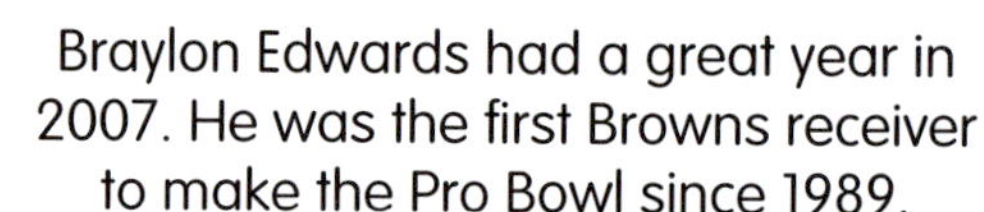

Braylon Edwards had a great year in 2007. He was the first Browns receiver to make the Pro Bowl since 1989.

BROWNS
17

Through the Years

1946

The Cleveland Browns begin play in the AAFC.

1949

The Browns win their fourth AAFC **championship**.

1950

The Browns win their first NFL championship.

1957

Fullback Jim Brown joins the team. He sets many records during his **career**.

1964

The Browns win their fourth NFL championship. They beat the Baltimore Colts 27–0.

1980

The team wins its first division title in nine years.

1985

Quarterback Bernie Kosar joins the team.

1987

The Browns play the New York Jets in the play-offs. It is one of the team's closest games. The Browns win 23–20 in double overtime.

1996–1998

The Cleveland Browns do not play for three seasons.

2014

A bullmastiff becomes the team's new **mascot**.

2015

The Browns wear newly designed team uniforms.

Postgame Recap

1. What is the name of the stadium where the Browns play home games?
   A. Metlife Stadium **B**. FirstEnergy Stadium **C**. Nissan Stadium

2. Who was the first coach of the Browns?
   A. Paul Brown
   B. Jim Brown
   C. Charlie Brown

3. Name 3 of the 16 Browns in the Pro Football Hall of Fame.

4. How many Super Bowls have the Browns played?
   A. 2
   B. 1
   C. 0

1. B. 2. A. 3. See page 15. 4. C.

Glossary

career a period of time spent in a certain job.

champion the winner of a championship, which is a game, a match, or a race held to find a first-place winner.

draft a system for professional sports teams to choose new players.

interception (ihn-tuhr-SEHP-shuhn) when a player catches a pass that was meant for the other team's player.

mascot something to bring good luck and help cheer on a team.

mentor someone who teaches or gives help and advice to a less experienced person.

retire to give up one's job.

rookie a first-year player in a professional sport.

Websites

To learn more about the NFL's Greatest Teams, visit **booklinks.abdopublishing.com**. These links are routinely monitored and updated to provide the most current information available.

Index